About the Author

Rachel Tsoumbakos has had several articles published through mainstream magazines and currently writes extensively for *The Inquisitr*.

Over the years, Rachel has been interested in many aspects of history. When studying a Library Studies diploma, she discovered just how much she enjoyed researching and has since used these skills in several of her novels. However, it was her work with *The Inquisitr* that brought her into the world of the Vikings and she has spent several years delving into the sagas of this culture as well as the history of the Viking Age.

Rachel lives with her husband, two kids, three cats and flock of chickens in the idyllic Yarra Ranges located near Melbourne, Australia. When she isn't writing, she is working on her cardio as she trains for the zombie apocalypse.

FIND RACHEL ONLINE:

Facebook:
http://www.facebook.com/rtsoumbakos
Twitter:
http://twitter.com/#!/mrszoomby
Blog:
http://racheltsoumbakos.wordpress.com
Newsletter:
bit.ly/RachelNL

RAGNAR AND THE WOMEN WHO LOVED HIM

RACHEL TSOUMBAKOS

RAGNAR AND THE WOMEN WHO LOVED HIM

Rachel Tsoumbakos

COPYRIGHT © 2017 by Rachel Tsoumbakos

MYRDDIN PUBLISHING GROUP

ALL RIGHTS RESERVED

Cover art: © Nejron | Dreamstime.com
Cover design: © Rachel Tsoumbakos
Time breaks designed using the Angerthas free font

For Mum.

Acknowledgements

I would like to thank David Cantrell for reading over this booklet. Your advice and eye for detail has been invaluable.

Contents

Think of me, I'll *think* of you.
Love me, I'll love you

~Anonymous, love message found on rune-sticks in Bergen, Norway.

Introduction

The Vikings and the sagas about them has always been a fascinating subject. They were a vicious breed, fierce, yet steeped in tradition and their own moral code. While many Vikings have captured the imagination of those who read about their feats, it seems the tales of Ragnar Lodbrok and his sons are some of the most recognised today thanks to History's television series, *Vikings*. Along with Ragnar, the women who loved him have created a fable that captures the imagination of people nowadays.

However, who was Ragnar Lodbrok and the women who loved him?

For many of you, this book has been found because your curiosity has been piqued as a result of watching this program and you want to find out more about Ragnar's story. Have you watched this series and fallen in love with the characters, but wondered how much of it is true? If so, this book is the perfect place to find out just how much of what you know about Ragnar's story thanks to the History Channel is correct. In my exploration, I will be referencing the History Channel's series and how they have helped to get the story right—and where they have gotten it wrong. *Vikings: Ragnar and the Women Who Loved Him* will delve into the stories that involve Ragnar Lodbrok and attempt to unravel the truth about him and the women he in which he was involved.

Vikings: Ragnar and the Women Who Loved Him will look at the history of Ragnar and discover who the women were that loved this famous Viking. It will also act as a complimentary introduction to the other books in the *Viking Secrets* series.

So, settle back and enjoy the ride.

PART ONE

THE FACTS

WHO WERE THE VIKINGS?

Originating in the Nordic section of Europe that includes Denmark, Finland, Iceland, Norway, and Sweden, they raided across Europe from the late 8th century through to the late 11th century AD. In fact, the very first recorded Viking raid can be pinpointed to an attack on the abbey at Lindisfarne on 8 June 793. According to historical documents of the time, a scholar working in Frankia wrote a letter describing the attack to the king of Northumbria and the bishop of Lindisfarne.

> "Pagans have desecrated God's sanctuary, shed the blood of saints around the altar, laid waste the house of our hope and trampled the bodies of saints like dung in the streets."[1]

Often we equate Vikings with violence. Known as barbarians who raped, pillaged, and looted wherever they set foot, popular culture has done little to explore beyond these stereotypes. Considering some of what is known about the Vikings has been written and handed down via Christian sources, it's possible that the Vikings were merely a casualty of religious propaganda rather than the bloodthirsty descriptives we have come to associate with them.

People from England, and the other countries they raided, also considered this group of people as non-Christian. This led to a further descriptive that fell under the umbrella term of

---

[1] Allott, S. (1974). *Alcuin of York: His Life and Letters*. York; letter no. 26, 36–8. and, also, Whitelock, D. (1979). *English Historical Documents,* vol. 1: c 550–1042. London: document no. 194, 778–9.

"Viking." So, when describing someone as a Viking, they could also be referring to their lack of a Christian belief system rather than their location.

For many, their lack of Christian beliefs is considered a reason why they were so brutal. However, it is possible the Vikings were a group of people that had very good reasons for doing what they did, and it might have had nothing to do with religion at all.

The Vikings were not actually a particular race from one country, but more a group of people that travelled from Scandinavia. Raiders and other groups that fell under this blanket title came from Norse countries such as Denmark, Norway, Sweden, and Iceland over a large period of time. They all shared a similar language as well as religious beliefs and culture. To outsiders, this made them all seem like the same people, and, in a way, they were. Nonetheless, each country had their own individual stories, some of which overlapped with others, but also, at times, pointed out their differences.

Regardless of why the Vikings were so violent, it is known they invaded various parts of Europe before branching out and raiding as far away as the Mediterranean, North Africa, the Middle East, Russia, and Central Asia.

The word "Viking," is generally considered by historians to come from the Scandinavian term "vikingr." To translate this term into English gives it the meaning of "pirate," or, alternatively, to mean those who are sea faring, or are a sea warrior, especially considering the word can be broken down further still into the Old Norse, "vik," meaning bay or creek. Therefore, it is possible this term has been translated in a way that has helped to perpetuate the villainy associated with them.

The term also represents a small percentage of the Norse population that later came to be known as "Vikings." However, for the sake of convenience in this section, I will be referring to the Norse populations of what became known as the Viking Age as "Vikings."

During the time of the Viking Age, Denmark, Finland, Norway, and Sweden were vastly different to the present day countries. Not only were some of these countries known by different names, but the boundaries were not set as firmly as they are today. Being a time when the Christians were converting and there was constant disagreement within the Viking settlements over who ruled each area, there was a certain fluidity to the borders. Added to this was the fact Vikings were known to fight among themselves over land parcels and rulership issues.

Nowadays, inheritance laws usually see land and property being passed down to a person's children, or next of kin. In the Viking Age, this was not always the way things were settled. While Vikings did pass their possessions on to their children, there were no set laws to enforce this. Many of the sagas talk of battles over land issues as well as land being inherited as a result of a person's lineage. In addition, the Vikings tended to divide their property between their children, rather than have the eldest son take possession of the vast majority of land. This, in turn, led to many squabbles over land as areas were divided up into smaller and smaller lots. This may be one of the factors that triggered the Viking Age.

The introduction of the Viking Age to the rest of Europe also occurred during what is known as the Medieval Warm Period. The period occurred around the same time many Icelandic Vikings migrated to Greenland. Their subsequent departure from Greenland also coincides with what is known as the Little Ice Age. Both of these events could indicate that Norse lands were changing as a result of the climate and the Vikings found the need to venture outside of their own countries in search of more suitable lands. Some of these Vikings could have tried places such as England and Ireland rather than migrate to Greenland. This is especially true if you consider that Greenland mostly managed to avoid temperature changes during the Medieval Warm Period and that may not be the reason why the Vikings moved away from the country when they did.

As well as the need for richer agricultural resources, we must also consider retribution against the Christian invasion that was attempting to extinguish their pagan beliefs. Initially, some Viking raids on Europe could be considered retaliation against the massive push at that time to convert everyone from their varying pagan beliefs to that of the more singular Christian belief system. Charlemagne's Saxon Wars occurred during this timeframe. This event saw Christianity enforced throughout Europe. Therefore, the Vikings were potentially pushing back against a culture that was foreign to them as the Christians advanced on the pagans during this time.

Regardless of why the Vikings invaded Europe, the fact is they arrived there and managed to integrate into many positions of power. While a rejection of Christianity could have been an initial catalyst for the Viking Age, it turned out the Viking's tenacity was due more to their adaptability rather than their aggression. The perfect example of this is Duke Rollo. This Viking assimilated into an invaded area and managed to become a leader there as a result of adapting to the local culture. Rollo was later baptized as Robert and became the first king of Normandy, a region in France. Over time, the Vikings managed to adapt and assimilate themselves into various countries and cultures, disappearing from their initial identity as "sea-faring warriors." So, while the Viking Age may have a fairly set end-time, the Vikings were still present, adding their own special flavours to the cultures they had joined.

For the sake of the argument, though, it is considered that the Viking Age ended in England with the Norman Conquest in 1066 at the Battle of Stamford Bridge. In Ireland, the era ended in 1171 with the capture of Dublin by Strongbow. 1263 saw the defeat of King Hákon Hákonarson at the Battle of Largs in Scotland which ended the age of the Vikings there. The Western Isles and the Isle of Man remained under Viking rule until 1266. Finally, Orkney and Shetland overthrew the king of Norway around 1469.

A MAP OF RAGNAR'S WORLD

The world that Ragnar lived in can been seen in the map below, using the common names for each area in the Viking Age as well as the places we now know them. Names in all capital letters, (i.e. SWEDEN) are the current titles. However, during the Viking Age, these areas were less defined or only known by the other name places indicated (i.e. Gotaland).

This map was originally developed from a public domain satellite image that was kindly provided by Koyos.

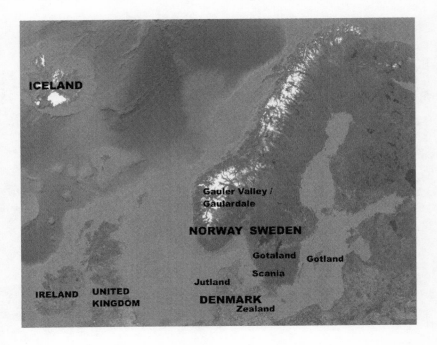

PART TWO

RAGNAR AND THE WOMEN WHO LOVED HIM

Ragnar

The legend involving Ragnar Lodbrok is a messy, murky one. It is unclear exactly when Ragnar even existed, if he was an amalgamation of several men known as Ragnar (or variants on that name), or merely a figment of the mythic parts of the sagas.

Ragnar Lothbrok is also known as Ragnar Lodbrok, Ragnar Lodbrog, Ragnar "Lodbrok" Sigurdsson or Ragnar Sigurdsson. Sigurdsson literally translates to the son of Sigurd. In one of the manuscripts that describes the Viking stories, the *Gesta Danorum*, Ragnar has his father listed as Siward Ring, and hence where the surname of Sigurdsson has originated.

The *Gesta Danorum* is a manuscript written by a Danish scholar sometime prior to 1208. Many scholars consider this book a work of fiction but in spite of this, it contains many accounts of the Viking tales we now know so can't be discredited as a source.

Because of potential fictional accounts such as the *Gesta Danorum* being blended with historical accounts of actual events, it is possible that several different people's deeds were amalgamated and then attributed to Ragnar. *The Sagas of Ragnar Lodbrok* by Ben Waggoner lists several different variants on the name that have been attributed to Ragnar Lodbrok over the years.[2] The *Frankish Annals* sees a man called Reginheri being mentioned. The stories attributing Ragnar Lodbrok's raids on

---

[2] Waggoner, B. (2009). *The Sagas of Ragnar Lodbrok*, Connecticut: The Troth, pp xxi-ii.

Paris can be linked back to this source. Ragnar might also be a man called Raginarius who was given land and a monastery by Charles the Bald in 840. While the sagas involving Ragnar Lodbrok don't specifically place Ragnar in Ireland, there is also evidence in Saxo's *Gesta Danorum* to suggest he could have raided there. It is also possible he could have died there sometime between 852 and 856 thanks to sources such as the *Chronicle of Ireland*. Another variant on his name that could be attributed to Ragnar is a Norse king called Ragnall. Although, it is possible this person could also be attributed to Reginheri and are not two separate people.

In recent culture, many would know Ragnar as Ragnar Lothbrok because of History Channel's *Vikings*. This character started out as a farmer, married to Lagertha, with two children; a girl, Gyda, and a son, Bjorn Ironside.

In the first season, Ragnar decides to buck against the wishes of the earl of Kattegat and venture into unchartered waters, which led him to England. Thus begins the first English invasion, when Ragnar's small fleet attacks the abbey at Lindisfarne. This is an event that has been historically recorded by English sources although not attributed to Ragnar specifically.

In the television series, this raid is the catalyst needed to catapult Ragnar into becoming the new earl of Kattegat, and, later, a king. It is a very interesting way to show the first Viking raid and to develop the story of both how the Viking Age begins, as well as to introduce how the legend of Ragnar Lodbrok first started. In the sagas, though, Ragnar's beginnings differ significantly. It is also highly unlikely the Vikings introduction to England was via a single raid.

While the tales about Ragnar do not really address his birth, it does introduce him from a very young age at points.

According to the *Gesta Danorum*, Ragnar was not a farmer, or from farming stock. His grandfather was a king, and Ragnar's father was in a position to follow into leadership. Then, as circumstance dictates, Ragnar is proclaimed king when he is very young. The other sagas involving Ragnar also describes him as royalty and not a commoner. However, by showing Ragnar as a commoner in the television series means viewers get to see how Vikings could progress from one station to another.

Ragnar's cunning and ability to rally those around him is indicated from an early age. Before he meets Lagertha in the *Gesta Danorum*, Ragnar had already proven his worth well before he became a man.

Prior to Ragnar's grandfather becoming king, another had been vying for the position. Ragnar's father was involved in many disputes in relation to who ruled the lands. In the meantime, locals claimed his son, Ragnar, as the rightful king, hoping this would add more weight to Siward's claim. Ragnar was a mere baby at the time, but they anticipated this would draw out those who were sluggish at backing Siward and they would, in turn, renew their support.

What ended up happening, though, was a retaliation that resulted in Siward's supporters being forced to choose between, as Saxo put it, "shame or peril."[3]

This is when the legend of Ragnar was first born. His name, translated from the Old Norse elements ragin- "counsel" and hari- "army" goes a long way in explaining the myth of Ragnar and how he is known for his way with people.

[3] Grammaticus, S. (2016). *The Danish History Books I-X*. [e-book]. Perennial Press. Available through: <https://www.amazon.com/Danish-History-Books-I-IX-ebook/dp/B01BRM2VFQ/> [Accessed: 2017].

Even as a boy, he managed to rally those around him. When those who were at counsel over what was to be done at this point, Ragnar offered his opinion. Considering the conundrum they were all in, they chose to hear the boy out. According to Saxo, Ragnar's advice was as follows.

> "The short bow shoots its shaft suddenly. Though it may seem the hardihood of a boy that I venture to forestall the speech of the elders, yet I pray you to pardon my errors, and be indulgent to my unripe words. Yet the counsellor of wisdom is not to be spurned, though he seem contemptible; for the teaching of profitable things should be drunk in with an open mind. Now it is shameful that we should be branded as deserters and runaways, but it is just as foolhardy to venture above our strength; and thus there is proved to be equal blame either way. We must, then, pretend to go over to the enemy, but, when a chance comes in our way, we must desert betimes. It will thus be better to forestall the wrath of our foe by reigned obedience than, by refusing it, to give him a weapon wherewith to attack us yet more harshly; for if we decline the sway of the stronger, are we not simply turning his arms against our own throat? Intricate devices are often the best nurse of craft. You need cunning to trap a fox."[4]

So, what does all that mean? Ragnar's plan was simple; they would play along until there was a moment when they could retaliate.

---

[4] Grammaticus, S. (2016). *The Danish History Books I-X.* [e-book]. Perennial Press. Available through: <https://www.amazon.com/Danish-History-Books-I-IX-ebook/dp/B01BRM2VFQ/> [Accessed: 2017].

Concerned at the fate of Ragnar if he were to be drawn into the battle, he was sent from Zealand to Norway to be raised. Ragnar's plans were still followed though and, in the process, Siward was mortally wounded and the young Ragnar became the king proper.

While Ragnar's tales are great, there is some dispute as to whether Ragnar was just one man, or, even existed at all. Hilda Ellis Davidson notes that book nine of the *Gesta Danorum* may actually be an amalgamation of several events that appear to be contradictory to each other.

Ellis also lists the following historical figures that may have had contributing factors in Ragnar's tales in her commentary on the *Gesta Danorum*:[5]

- King Horik I
- King Reginfrid
- A king of Denmark known to have come into conflict with Harald Klak (this could be the Harald mentioned earlier involving the battle where Lagertha triumphed.)
- Reginherus (also known as Reginheri), a person who invaded Paris in the middle of the ninth century
- Rognvald of the *Chronicle of Ireland*
- The father of some of the Viking leaders who led the Great Heathen Army in 865, although he was never named as such in the *Anglo Saxon Chronicle*

Regardless of Ragnar's authenticity, the medieval sources involving Ragnar Lodbrok include the following:

---

[5] Grammaticus, S., Davidson, H. E., and Fisher, P. (1979). *The History of the Danes: Books I-IX*. Woodbridge: D. S. Brewer.

- Book nine of the *Gesta Danorum*
- *The Tale of Ragnar's Sons* also known as the *Ragnarssona þáttr* saga
- *The Tale of Ragnar Lodbrok*, a sequel to the *Völsunga* saga
- *The Ragnarsdrápa*, which is a fragmented skaldic poem attributed to the 9th-century poet Bragi Boddason
- *The Krákumál*, a 12th-century Icelandic poem which is also known as Ragnar's death-song
- *Anglo Saxon Chronicle*, which was written during events occurring in England at the time
- *Heimskringla*, which is also known as *A History of the Norse Kings*

For many who are new to the stories about Ragnar Lodbrok, it is the women who he was involved with that help to shape his character and flesh out his stories. In particular, thanks to History Channel's *Vikings*, it is Ragnar's relationship with the shield maiden, Lagertha that is most often researched when first delving into the world of the Vikings. However, Ragnar's time with Lagertha is only ever mentioned in the *Gesta Danorum*. After they parted ways he continued to do many great deeds. In fact, it wasn't until after he and Lagertha separated that he obtained the nickname Lodbrok.

In the ninth book of the *Gesta Danorum*, it is explained that Ragnar became infatuated with a woman once again—this time Thora Borgarhjört. In order to marry Thora, Ragnar had to defeat dangerous beasts that Thora had raised and were causing trouble across the land. Her father, Herodd, welcomes anyone to step forth and kill the animals in return for his daughter's hand in marriage.

Herodd is also known by the names: Herraud, Herröðr, Herrud, Herothus or Heroth, and the earl of Götaland. In Ben Waggoner's *The Sagas of Ragnar Lodbrok*, he is also known as Gautric,[6] who is a baron of Gautland (Gautland is another name for Götaland). Regardless of his name, in each translation, he insists that anyone who slays the beasts can wed his daughter.

The animals he had to battle this time around were dangerous serpents that Thora had raised herself.

Ragnar, being an intelligent man who was happy to wait patiently, observed many men attempting to kill the animals. From this, he formulated a plan to cover the lower part of his body in thick, shaggy hides that the snakes would not be able to pierce. He also covered these hairy breeches in tar and sand, as added protection.

It was these pants, plus a shield to protect him from the serpents' venom, that allowed Ragnar to get close enough to slay the animals and win Thora's hand. King Herodd was so impressed—and amused—with Ragnar's hairy pants that he gave Ragnar the nickname, Loðbrók, which translates into "Hairy-Breeks" or, more commonly, "hairy breeches."

Once Ragnar was victorious, their union, according to the *Tale of Ragnar's Sons*, produced two sons, Eirik and Agnar. Both would die in battle. However, by that point in the tale, Thora had also died.

Along with Thora's sons, others are mentioned in the *Gesta Danorum*, namely: Radbard, Dunwat, Siward, Biorn, and Iwar.

---

[6] Waggoner, B. (2009). *The Sagas of Ragnar Lodbrok*. Connecticut: The Troth, p. 61.

> "By [Thora] he begot two nobly-gifted sons, Radbard and Dunwat. These also had brothers—Siward, Biorn, Agnar, and Iwar."[7]

It seems unclear what Saxo meant by this. Could Ragnar have had six sons to Thora? Or, perhaps, considering the first two are noted as being "nobly-gifted," it could be suggested that Ragnar bore four illegitimate sons during his time with Thora. While some of these sons names are often attributed to another wife of Ragnar's, it is suspected this part of Saxo's story is an amalgamation of Ragnar's wives.

In regard to how many children Ragnar sired overall, the list is vast. While he is known to have had three children with Lagertha and at least two with Thora in the *Gesta Danorum*, he is also known to have had children with another wife, Aslaug. Along with these legitimate children, Saxo also saw him bear a child, Ubbe (sometimes written as Ubbi), to the daughter of Esbern.

The Saga of Ragnar Lodbrok fragment also makes mention of another son called Rognvald.

Along with this, several texts also reference a son, Halfdan. Although, this sibling tie is implied and does not directly state Halfdan is the son of Ragnar Lodbrok. Either, Halfdan is an illegitimate son of Ragnar, or he is known as a son due to his loyalty. Alternatively, it is possible Halfdan could be Hvitserk, another one of Ragnar's sons.

As can been seen, between the varying sagas involving Ragnar, his children are often mixed up or incorrectly attributed depending on the story or fragment.

---

[7] Grammaticus, S. (2016). *The Danish History Books I-X.* [e-book]. Perennial Press. Available through: <https://www.amazon.com/Danish-History-Books-I-IX-ebook/dp/B01BRM2VFQ/> [Accessed: 2017].

As a result of this, the other sons mentioned by Saxo seem likely to be the sons attributed to Aslaug in the *Tale of Ragnar's Sons*. Ivar the Boneless, Bjorn Ironsides, Hvitserk and Sigurd are listed as sons of Aslaug to Ragnar in this fragment. As well, the *Tale of Ragnar's Sons* mentions Sigurd along with the prevailing story involving a snake pattern in his eye, something Saxo also references.

It is possible, by Saxo listing Aslaug's children as Thora's, he either incorrectly credited these children to her, did not know about the saga involving Aslaug, or—as mentioned prior— amalgamated stories involving Ragnar's wives. This is also the section in the *Gesta Danorum* where there is a significant timeframe issue involving Ragnar, his children and his marriages. Potentially, it could also indicate Ragnar married Aslaug prior to Lagertha, or in between his divorce to her and subsequent marriage to Thora and for whatever reason Saxo left Aslaug's story out of the *Gesta Danorum*. Regardless, in the *Gesta Danorum* it appears that Ragnar divorced Lagertha and immediately began his pursuit of Thora.

Aslaug's marriage to Ragnar is noted in some of the other stories and sagas involving Ragnar, most notably, the *Saga of Ragnar Lodbrok* and the *Tale of Ragnar's Sons*. Her marriage is often accepted to occur after the death of Thora, which would make Aslaug Ragnar's third wife in the *Gesta Danorum*. In the *Tale of Ragnar's Sons*, she is listed as his second wife as Lagertha does not appear in this saga fragment. In both instances, Aslaug is considered the woman Ragnar marries after Thora. This means the ninth book of the *Gesta Danorum* contains some inconsistencies.

While it is widely accepted Aslaug married a man named Ragnar, it is also a possibility she did not wed Ragnar Lodbrok. In fact, some sources suggest that Aslaug lived as long as three hundred and fifty years before Ragnar Lodbrok and could indicate two different men named Ragnar in the saga fragments involving him and the *Gesta Danorum*.

In the *Gesta Danorum*, Siward is an adult, indicating Ragnar has married Aslaug already and bore Siward to Ragnar. This story also gives the reason as to why Siward is also known as Sigurd Snake-in-the-Eye, so it can be assumed this Siward is definitely Aslaug's son. However, it seems Thora is still alive and Ragnar is still married to her at this point in time.

Ragnar and Aslaug (also known as Kraka, in the Viking stories) met much like in History Channel's *Vikings*. Having been spotted bathing by Ragnar's men, Ragnar's interest was piqued and he demanded they meet but she was "neither dressed nor undressed, neither hungry nor full and neither alone nor in company."[8] Aslaug arrived wearing a net, eating an onion and accompanied by a dog. Ragnar was so impressed he proposed marriage. Aslaug, like many of the women Ragnar found attractive, set him a task before they could marry. He would have to complete his current mission in Norway before they wed, or even before she would consent to have sex with him. Ragnar did this and they were married afterwards. Aslaug then went on to produce the sons mentioned previously; the famous Vikings, Ivar the Boneless, Hvitserk, Bjorn Ironside and Sigurd Snake-in-the-Eye.

While Aslaug is much maligned in the television series and their marriage ends up being loveless, in the sagas it is a different story. Their marriage not only produces many sons but appears to be successful in many other aspects. While not explicitly said, it appears Aslaug loved Ragnar right up until the

---

[8] Waggoner, B. (2009). *The Sagas of Ragnar Lodbrok*. Connecticut: The Troth, p.9.

end and the same could be said in regard to Ragnar and his affections for her.

However, of all Ragnar's relationships, arguably, it is Thora he was most attached to according to Saxo's ninth book of the *Gesta Danorum*. When she died of an illness, Ragnar was greatly distressed.

> "Meantime Thora, the bride of Ragnar, perished of a violent malady, which caused infinite trouble and distress to the husband, who dearly loved his wife."[9]

After Thora's death, Ragnar decided to put this misery to good use and found solace in exercise and hard work.

It was this event that led him to create an army consisting of those which each family thought were too contemptible or lazy to be of much service to them, be it son or slave. This was something he had tried out to a lesser degree during the battle Lagertha helped him with, employing those considered too old or weak to help him when he wasn't sure his army would be big enough. The army was used to prove that the "feeblest of the Danish race were better than the strongest men of other nations."[10]

Aslaug predicted Ragnar's demise if he left once more for England. Ragnar travelled anyway. The common story surrounding his death was that he was captured there by King Aelle and thrown into a pit of venomous snakes. It was a fate from which Aslaug nearly saved him. She had commissioned a

---

[9] Grammaticus, S. (2016). *The Danish History Books I-X*. [e-book]. Perennial Press. Available through: <https://www.amazon.com/Danish-History-Books-I-IX-ebook/dp/B01BRM2VFQ/> [Accessed: 2017].

[10] Grammaticus, S. (2016). *The Danish History Books I-X*. [e-book]. Perennial Press. Available through: <https://www.amazon.com/Danish-History-Books-I-IX-ebook/dp/B01BRM2VFQ/> [Accessed: 2017].

magical vest that was blessed by the gods in order to safeguard him. When King Aelle realised Ragnar's clothing was protecting him, he ordered the removal of it, and Ragnar perished.

The death song of Ragnar Lodbrok, the *Krákumál*, describes how Ragnar valiantly sung as he died, ready and willing to enter Valhalla after he perished.

> "It gladdens me to know that Baldr's father [Odin] makes ready the benches for a banquet. Soon we shall be drinking ale from the curved horns. The champion who comes into Odin's dwelling [Valhalla] does not lament his death. I shall not enter his hall with words of fear upon my lips. The Æsir will welcome me. Death comes without lamenting. Eager am I to depart. The Dísir summon me home, those whom Odin sends for me [valkyries] from the halls of the Lord of Hosts. Gladly shall I drink ale in the high-seat with the Æsir. The days of my life are ended. I laugh as I die."[11]

Varying sources place Ragnar's death sometime around 840 to 865. However, Ragnar's sons avenged his death when their Great Heathen Army attacked in 865 and it is suggested by some sources that the Great Heathen Army killed Aelle in the battle at York in 867. Symeon's *Historia Regum Anglorum* gives the date for this battle and Aelle's subsequent death as 21 March, 867. The account is described below.

> "In those days, the nation of the Northumbrians had violently expelled from the kingdom the rightful king of

---

[11] Symeon of Durham; Stevenson, J. translator (1855). *The Historical Works of Simeon of Durham*. Church Historians of England, volume III, part II. Seeley's.

their nation, Osbryht by name, and had placed at the head of the kingdom a certain tyrant, named Alla [Aelle]. When the pagans came upon the kingdom, the dissension was allayed by divine counsel and the aid of the nobles. King Osbryht and Alla, having united their forces and formed an army, came to the city of York; on their approach the multitude of the shipmen immediately took flight. The Christians, perceiving their flight and terror, found that they themselves were the stronger party. They fought upon each side with much ferocity, and both kings fell. The rest who escaped made peace with the Danes."[12]

And so, with the death of Ragnar, and the consequences of his killer described, it is time to conclude this section and turn, instead, to the women who loved him.

---

[12] Simeon of Durham. (1130). *Symeonis Dunelmensis Opera et collectanea.* and, Hodgson-Hinde, J. (1868). Making of America Project.

THE WIVES

ℒAGERTHA

The story of Lagertha and Ragnar's romance is a strange one. It is wedged in between his other wives in one small section of text from Saxo Grammaticus' ninth book of the *Gesta Danorum*. Nowhere else is Lagertha mentioned, either in the *Gesta Danorum*, or in other manuscripts, indicating Lagertha's story might not even be real.

Yet, the story has become as tenacious as Lagertha herself. While there may be more recorded texts of Ragnar's other wives, Aslaug and Thora, for many people, the most famous Vikings of all are Lagertha and Ragnar.

Today, Lagertha is currently a Viking character who has gained a lot of attention due to History Channel's portrayal of her in their historical drama, *Vikings*. Prior to the television series, she was often known as a fierce shield maiden.

While it is unclear whether shield maidens existed in Viking times, archaeological evidence is now starting to side with the stories about these battle-ready women. For a long time, many scholars had assumed shield maidens were a figment of the imagination of those who finally wrote down the sagas. However, a recent re-evaluation of the bodies found in an old Viking burial on English soil suggest that more women than initially thought might have been involved with the battle aspects of Viking life as raids occurred outside of Scandinavia.

Many female viewers of History Channel's *Vikings* seem to identify with the character of Lagertha because of the strong female role she plays within the program. The character is not only a pivotal role, but, as a female, her warrior inclinations are not seen as secondary to her maternal functions. Considered a shield maiden, Lagertha regularly fights among the men during Viking raids. She has also managed to claim her own Earldom.

In History Channel's *Vikings*, we see a character who was the first wife of Ragnar. Even though their marriage ends in divorce after Ragnar gets Princess Aslaug pregnant, it is obvious that their relationship is a deep one. Over the years, the pair keep in touch as well as fight side by side when required.

The relationship in this series saw a young farming family grow into a power couple that ruled in different locations based on their own strengths. For Lagertha it is her fighting skills, and, for Ragnar, it is not only his ability as a warrior, but also his insight and being able to charm people and pit sides against each other to his own advantage and gain.

In an age where it is important to find strong, positive role models for girls, Lagertha has arrived at just the right moment to capture the imagination of women and girls alike. Not only does she rule on her own merits, but also she was involved in, arguably, the show's greatest love story. Yet, she is not defined by this love story alone, like many women in other television series are. In the television show, Lagertha fights alongside the men and is involved in many storylines that are not merely romantic plot devices. She is in control of her own life, even if she does think it is fated by the gods and will act with courage in response.

The ninth book of the *Gesta Danorum* reveals that Lagertha was a noble woman who was taken hostage and placed into prostitution—along with a group of noblewomen—after the Norwegian king, Siward, was slain by King Fro of Sweden.

Upon hearing of Siward's death and the fate of these women, Ragnar prepares to rescue them. It is an insult against his family, after all, and something had to be done immediately.

When he approaches the brothel, many of the shamed women dress as men and rush to Ragnar's camp. They are willing to join him in battle to defeat the King of Sweden, choosing death over dishonour.

Lagertha was among these women who dressed up as men and fought alongside Ragnar. Her first appearance to Ragnar is described as follows.

> "Among them was Ladgerda, a skilled amazon, who, though a maiden, had the courage of a man, and fought in front among the bravest with her hair loose over her shoulders. All-marvelled at her matchless deeds, for her locks flying down her back betrayed that she was a woman."[13]

Ragnar was fascinated by Lagertha, accrediting her with the battle being won thanks to the "might of one woman."[14] Then, as he tended to do in many of the stories involving himself and women, he pursued her relentlessly.

Lagertha was not one to be easily swayed by a man, though. Saxo describes her as spurning "his mission in her heart, but feign[ing] compliance."

At first, as a result of this, she played with his affections by sending false replies to his many messages that suggested he

[13] Grammaticus, S. (2016). *The Danish History Books I-X*. [e-book]. Perennial Press. Available through: <https://www.amazon.com/Danish-History-Books-I-IX-ebook/dp/B01BRM2VFQ/> [Accessed: 2017].

[14] Grammaticus, S. (2016). *The Danish History Books I-X*. [e-book]. Perennial Press. Available through: <https://www.amazon.com/Danish-History-Books-I-IX-ebook/dp/B01BRM2VFQ/> [Accessed: 2017].

would "gain his desires," if he were to approach. To thwart his advances, she had a bear and a dog placed in front of her dwelling. Ragnar was confronted with these obstacles after crossing the sea to approach her. Confidently, he slew the beasts and Lagertha had no option but to marry Ragnar afterwards.

It is unclear from this early section of the ninth book whether Lagertha was interested in Ragnar or not. Considering the ordeal she had previously encountered with Fro and being thrust into a life of prostitution, it seems likely she may not have been interested in pursuit by another man. Although, because marriage, at that time, was usually geared more towards gain than love, this notion is established by the present-day assumption that marriage should be based on emotional needs.

Lagertha is considered of noble blood, so this means she would have been prepared to marry again, or even to be coerced by her family into another marriage. In addition, considering Ragnar's position, their union would be a good one for her to make socially. However, by having Lagertha obviously playing with Ragnar's affections suggests some sort of conflict; be it her family wanting her to remarry, a genuine lack of interest in Ragnar, or perhaps even her having genuine feelings for Ragnar yet feeling like she should push him away after her previous ordeal. If we place Lagertha, once again, within the present day in regard to the sex trade, perhaps she even considered herself damaged goods and not worthy of someone like Ragnar. Unfortunately, we will likely never know as Saxo is not forthcoming in the reasons why Lagertha toyed with Ragnar in regard to her affections.

While she may have objected to his advances at first, their marriage appeared to be contented at the start. Three children were born to their union: two unnamed girls, and a son, Fridleif.

Their life after that point was happy for a time that Saxo records as three years. However, those in the surrounding Jutland, which nowadays is a part of Denmark, were critical of Ragnar's rule. Ragnar was supposed to be the ruler of Jutland at that point in time, but the assumption was made that Ragnar would never return to them from Zealand (another part of what is known today as Denmark), where he and Lagertha were currently residing.

As a result of this, the Jutlanders joined with Skania (known today as Sweden) and planned an attack on Zealand. Ragnar managed to get wind of this attack and retaliated with thirty of his own ships, crushing the two groups and regaining his power there.

In the *Gesta Danorum* it is unclear how long these battles took, but, at the end of them, Ragnar had grown tired of Lagertha and chose to divorce her on account of the fact that she had "long ago set the most savage beasts to destroy him." It is with a certain irony that the woman he now set his sights on, Thora (also known as Þóra Borgarhjǫrtr or Thora Borgarhjört), the daughter of King Herodd, would also have obstacles in front of her.

While Ragnar and Lagertha parted ways at this point and Ragnar did manage to win Thora's hand in marriage, the story of Lagertha and Ragnar is not yet over.

After Ragnar divorced Lagertha and married Thora, those in Jutland and Skania were not happy with Ragnar again. And, once more, it was because he was spending time with his new wife rather than being at home and ruling over his lands. As a result, the regions decided to disallow his title, giving it instead to another ruler called Harald.

Once Ragnar was alerted to this, he immediately reached out to all of his allies in order to go up against the resistance. Of these allies, Lagertha was included. This indicates that while Ragnar may have divorced her, they were still on relatively good speaking terms. Or, at least, their divorce was not as bitter as one might expect when the husband decides to pursue another woman. Ragnar, it seems, has also forgotten the reason he divorced Lagertha was because he mistrusted her for pitting dangerous animals against him. Alternatively, he might have decided that he needed such a fierce woman on his side and not against him.

Lagertha obliged Ragnar's request for assistance. Since their divorce, she had remarried, so her husband and her son, Fridleif, also accompany her. Saxo describes the event in the ninth book of the *Gesta Danorum* as follows.

> "Ladgerda, whose early love still flowed deep and steadfast, hastily sailed off with her husband and her son. She brought herself to offer a hundred and twenty ships to the man who had once put her away."[15]

Other than Saxo noting Lagertha was married, very little is known about this new husband. Regardless, Ragnar did not yet know she was sending such a huge convoy and was prepared to round up anyone who would support him. That included the sick and the elderly in amongst the able-bodied men.

After Lagertha arrived, a battle ensued. Saxo describes how Lagertha, once again, came to Ragnar's aid when most needed and it seemed like hope was lost.

---

[15] Grammaticus, S. (2016). *The Danish History Books I-X*. [e-book]. Perennial Press. Available through: <https://www.amazon.com/Danish-History-Books-I-IX-ebook/dp/B01BRM2VFQ/> [Accessed: 2017].

"Ladgerda, who had a matchless spirit though a delicate frame, covered by her splendid bravery the inclination of the soldiers to waver. For she made a sally about, and flew round to the rear of the enemy, taking them unawares, and thus turned the panic of her friends into the camp of the enemy.[16]"

It is often this passage that is used to help support the notion that Lagertha is, in fact, a version of the goddess, Thorgerd. This goddess is often associated with the valkyries, who decided the fate of those in battle. The fact Lagertha managed to turn the whole battle around in this passage, suggests she could well be like a valkyrie who has changed the fates of those in battle.

Regardless of whether Lagertha was a human or a goddess, something must have changed for Lagertha after this battle as her story takes an abrupt turn of events. Saxo does not elaborate why these events happen, and fails, yet again, to mention the name of Lagertha's husband, but Lagertha decides she has had enough of him.

"Ladgerda, when she had gone home after the battle, murdered her husband … in the night with a spear-head, which she had hid in her gown. Then she usurped the whole of his name and sovereignty; for this most presumptuous dame thought it pleasanter to rule without her husband than to share the throne with him.[17]"

---

[16] Grammaticus, S. (2016). *The Danish History Books I-X*. [e-book]. Perennial Press. Available through: <https://www.amazon.com/Danish-History-Books-I-IX-ebook/dp/B01BRM2VFQ/> [Accessed: 2017].

[17] Grammaticus, S. (2016). *The Danish History Books I-X*. [e-book]. Perennial Press. Available through: <https://www.amazon.com/Danish-History-Books-I-IX-ebook/dp/B01BRM2VFQ/> [Accessed: 2017].

And, this is where Lagertha's tale ends in Saxo's *Gesta Danorum*. If you would like to find out more about Lagertha and Ragnar's story, you can do so in my book, *Vikings: The Truth about Lagertha and Ragnar*. This book delves into not only the historical aspects of their story, whether shield maidens are real, and whether Lagertha was really a valkyrie, but it presents Lagertha and Ragnar's love story in a fictional retelling of the ninth book of the *Gesta Danorum*.

While Ragnar and Lagertha's love story is now told, what of the other women who loved this famous Viking?

THORA

In History Channel's *Vikings*, Ragnar is married to Lagertha and then is divorced by her when he gets the princess, Aslaug, pregnant. These two women are the only wives of the famous Viking in the television series. However, according to the sagas, Ragnar had three wives. Thora, who isn't mentioned in the series is the reason he obtained his famous nickname, Lodbrok (translated to Lothbrok in the television series).

According to the *Gesta Danorum*, Thora might have also been Ragnar's one true love. Unlike Lagertha's tale, Thora's is included in more than just the one manuscript, which gives us more scope when it comes to the validity of this relationship.

Thora, also known as Þóra Borgarhjǫrtr, Thora Borgarhjört, and Thora Town-Hart, is mentioned in several medieval texts. *The Saga of Ragnar Lodbrok and his Sons* also notes that Thora is called Fortress-Hart. Hart, being an old word for deer, indicates that Thora excelled in her beauty in the same way a deer was held in higher esteem over other animals at the time. In other words, her beauty and high standing made her the best catch out of all the women in the land.

Not only does Thora appear alongside Lagertha in the *Gesta Danorum*, but the *Saga of Ragnar Lodbrok and his Sons*, the *Tale of Ragnar's Sons*. An ancient list of Swedish kings also mentions Thora.

Lagertha may have been considered of undefined noble stock. However, it is known that Thora is the daughter of King Herodd (also known as Herraud, Herrauðr, or Herrud) the earl of Gotaland, which is an area in present-day Sweden. In spite of class, like Lagertha, Ragnar has to vie for Thora's attention.

Being a princess, Thora appeared to be spoiled by her father from a very early age, with the *Saga of Ragnar Lodbrok and his Sons* mentioning the fact Herodd brought his daughter a gift every day. One of these gifts, a heather snake—or two of them, depending on the telling—is the reason Ragnar ends up winning Thora's hand in marriage. While the stories involving this tale tell of Herodd giving his daughter a snake, or snakes, one saga, *Bósa saga ok Herrauðs*, sees Herodd receive a vulture's egg. He later gives this egg to Thora. When it hatches, it reveals the snake.

While the gifted snake starts out fairly innocuous, Thora relishes the task of looking after the creature and gave it extra special treatment as a result. She placed the heather snake inside a small box and fed it every day, placing a gold coin underneath it with every meal she provided.

The snake grew and grew. When it is too big for the box, Thora allowed the animal to rest around the outside of the box. With all the continued feeding, the snake continued to grow and becomes large enough to wrap around Thora's bower.

It is at this point in the tale that the snake is now being referred to as a serpent and locals are also calling it a pest as a result of its sheer size. This serpent becomes so big that it requires an ox every day as nourishment. The *Gesta Danorum*, at this point also refers to the animal as a lindworm, which, according to medieval literature, is a creature similar to a dragon. The only person who will approach Herrod's residence now is Thora. Herodd, disheartened by the fact no one will visit him and that the creatures were scorching his lands, decides the snake needs to go. He declares to all who will listen that the man who kills the serpent will have his daughter's hand in marriage.

Ragnar, at this time is either still married to Lagertha or just recently divorced as a result of his infatuation with Thora. Either way, their break up is a direct result of Ragnar's interest in Thora. Once Herodd announces he wants Thora's serpent killed, however, Ragnar is considered a free man and begins to devise a plan to win Thora's hand.

Ragnar fashions a pair of shaggy pants that he covers in tar and sand according to one tale. The *Gesta Danorum* does not see his pants being tarred, but this manuscript does see Ragnar also donning a dress stuffed with hair and dousing it in water that freezes over night to further protect him from Thora's snake. Regardless of which description is true, Ragnar manages to wear enough clothing to protect himself from the venom of the lindworm and slay the pest.

Ragnar breaks off his sword in the beast and it is not until he comes forward later, in a Cinderella-like event and shows that his broken sword fits the fragment left in the animal perfectly, that Ragnar is declared victorious.

When Herodd finally finds out that Ragnar has completed the task and sees what he wore in order to do so, gives him the moniker "Lodbrok." This word translates to "shaggy pants" or hair breeches" echoing the fact that Ragnar wore thick clothing to defeat the animal.

After this, Herodd allowed Ragnar and Thora to marry. It is unclear from the fragments of stories involving these two how Thora felt about this arrangement. While she is described many times as beautiful, not a lot has been recorded about how she felt about her husband. None of the sagas mentioning this story explains how Thora felt about Ragnar killing her pet snake.

Neither is it recorded how she felt about her new husband, one she had likely never met prior to their marriage.

We also know that Thora begot two sons to Ragnar: Radbard and Dunwat. In other sagas, however, her sons are listed as being named Eirik and Agnar. Despite differing names, it is consistent that this marriage produced two children. While this is no indicator of how Thora thought about Ragnar, it does prove they were, at least, intimate.

Ragnar, on the other hand appeared enamoured by her. The *Saga of Ragnar Lodbrok and his Sons* insists that Ragnar "loved Thora greatly."[18] This is further attested to when Thora dies suddenly of an unnamed but violent malady. Ragnar, so despondent by his wife's death, takes to raiding rather than ruling in order to work through his grief. The *Gesta Danorum* goes so far as to say that Thora's death "caused infinite trouble and distress to the husband, who loved his wife dearly."[19]

While Ragnar may have loved Thora immensely, his raiding is what leads him to find his next wife, Aslaug.

---

[18] [18] Grammaticus, S. (2016). *The Danish History Books I-X.* [e-book]. Perennial Press. Available through: <https://www.amazon.com/Danish-History-Books-I-IX-ebook/dp/B01BRM2VFQ/> [Accessed: 2017].
 [19] [19] Grammaticus, S. (2016). *The Danish History Books I-X.* [e-book]. Perennial Press. Available through: <https://www.amazon.com/Danish-History-Books-I-IX-ebook/dp/B01BRM2VFQ/> [Accessed: 2017].

ASLAUG

As previously mentioned, Aslaug is considered Ragnar's second wife in History Channel's *Vikings*, behind the shield maiden, Lagertha. For many fans of the television show, Aslaug is the wife who stole Ragnar away from Lagertha and made her life a misery. To say there is no love lost among viewers for Aslaug is an understatement.

In the single story involving Lagertha, the *Gesta Danorum*, Aslaug doesn't even exist. Although, her sons do, indicating the author of this manuscript, Saxo Grammaticus, may have known at least a little of Aslaug's tale.

When Thora and Ragnar marry, it is mentioned that they have two sons, Eirik and Agnar, who are listed as brothers alongside Siward, Bjorn, Agnar, and Ivar. While Agnar has been attributed in other sagas as being Thora's son, the other three boys have usually been attributed as being Aslaug's sons to Ragnar.

There are also other stories that attest to Aslaug being the wife of Ragnar Lodbrok. Aslaug is mentioned in the *Edda*, the *Völsunga saga*, the *Saga of Ragnar Lodbrok and his Sons*, and the *Tale of Ragnar's Sons*. The Edda and the Völsunga saga only give a brief mention Aslaug, so most of her story falls to the remaining sagas listed.

Aslaug has a very tough upbringing, thanks to the death of her parents, the famous dragon slayer, Sigurd, and the shield maiden and potential valkyrie, Brynhildr, Aslaug is fostered by Heimir, a man who had his own kingdom but gave up his power in order to protect Aslaug. He did this by hiding the child inside his harp case and travelling around the countryside as if he were a beggar.

Heimir would only bring Aslaug out of her hiding spot if they were far away from prying eyes. If Aslaug were sad, he would play his harp to make her happy again, potential evidence to suggest it was a horrible existence for the child.

After travelling like this for some while, Heimir came to a farm in Norway called Spangareid. This place was owned by Aki and Grima, a couple who are described as incredibly ugly, in particular, Grima.

While Heimir has been very careful to hide not only his foster daughter but also his wealth up to this point, he is a little careless at this farm and Grima spies expensive cloth dangling from the harp case and a gold ring on Heimir's finger. She then devises a plan that sees her husband kill Heimir so they can take his treasures. To their surprise, after Aki kills Heimir, they discover a child within the harp case as well as his riches.

Seeing this as opportunistic, Grima decides they will pretend Aslaug is their daughter and put her to work on the farm so they will not have to toil as much as they used to. As Aki points out, Aslaug is way too beautiful to be considered a daughter of Grima. Hence, his wife cuts off Aslaug's hair, coats it in tar, and renames her Kraka, after her own mother. Kraka is then set to work for the remainder of her childhood. As she grows up, there is some indication that Kraka becomes a little unruly. Nothing too serious though, but, when Ragnar's men arrive at Spangareid, Grima makes a mention of this.

While Grima has done her best to make Kraka appear unattractive, when her services are offered to Ragnar's men, who need help to bake their bread, his men burn their bread because they can't stop gazing at the attractive woman. When they return to Ragnar, they explain this to their king and Ragnar insists he needs to see her. He sends a message to Kraka asking that she meet him. Ragnar also sets out a riddle for her to solve. He asks that she be brought to him neither clad nor unclad, neither fasting nor eating, and neither alone nor in company.

Kraka, being clever, devised a way to achieve this task. She wraps herself in a net and let her hair hang down to cover her virtue. She brings a leek with her that she took a bite out of so she was neither hungry nor sated. Finally, she takes a dog with her so she can claim she was accompanied, yet no person was with her.

Ragnar was impressed with Kraka after this and he relentlessly pursued her. Kraka, however, insisted he continue on with his planned voyage and return to Norway if he didn't find someone more suited to him in the meantime.

Ragnar, of course, returned after his journey and laid claim to Aslaug. She accompanied him on his ship but insisted her virtue remain intact by having them sleep in separate beds. Then, when they were eventually wed, she issued a final warning to Ragnar. She insisted they couldn't consummate their marriage for three nights after their wedding or she would bear a child that had no bones in his legs. Ragnar ignored this warning and their marriage was consummated on the first night. Thus, Ivar the Boneless was conceived.

Over the course of their marriage, there seemed to be happiness. The *Saga of Ragnar Lodbrok and his Sons* calls their marriage good and loving. Other sons are also born: Bjorn, Hvitserk, Rognvald, and Sigurd, a further indication this marriage was prosperous.

However, when Ragnar made a trip to visit Eystein, the king of Sweden, he became betrothed to his daughter, Ingibjorg. The reasoning behind this was that everyone still thought

Kraka to be a peasant's daughter and beneath Ragnar's standing.

When Ragnar returned home, Kraka confronted him about this betrothal and finally revealed her true identity. While her story seemed fanciful and unable to be proven, she insisted it was true and declared their next child born would have the symbol of a snake in his eye. If this proved true, then so must her story.

After some time, their son was born. He certainly did appear to have a snake in his eye and Ragnar announced to everyone that Kraka was really Aslaug, the daughter of the famous Sigurd and Brynhildr. His betrothal to Ingibjorg was called off after which led to conflict between Ragnar and Eystein. This disagreement ultimately resulted in the death of his sons to Thora.

This event seems to indicate that Aslaug and Ragnar could have been besotted with each other. After all, Ragnar was happy to stop his betrothal to Ingibjorg once it was proven who Kraka was. Although, the texts could indicate that the reason Ragnar was happy with this news was because it placed Aslaug in a higher standing than Eystein's daughter. Aslaug, on the other hand, begged Ragnar to stop the betrothal and only revealed her story to him once it seemed likely he would leave her. So, potentially, Aslaug loved Ragnar more than he loved her. In any event, they stayed together afterwards until Ragnar's death.

In fact, Ragnar's death is another place where it would be said Aslaug was deeply in love with Ragnar. After the deaths of Thora's sons, his other sons banded together and helped to defeat King Eystein. When Ragnar heard this news he became jealous of his sons fame and tried to outdo them. He devised a plan, which—if successful—would see Ragnar conquer England using only two ships.

When Aslaug heard of this foolish plan, she made him a shirt that would protect him from injury. Ragnar took this shirt and wore it to England. When he left Aslaug behind, it is said that she was greatly distressed by his departure.

Ragnar made it to England. When King Aelle captured him and threw him into the snake pit, no injury resulted. Finally, Aelle ordered Ragnar's shirt be removed and it is at this point that Ragnar succumbs to the snakes.

If you are intrigued by the stories involving Aslaug and would like to find out more about how they differ from the television series, my book, *Vikings: The Truth about Aslaug and Ragnar* delves into this further. In particular, it covers their love story, whether Aslaug was secretly infatuated with one of her stepsons, and, ultimately, Ragnar's death at the hands of King Aelle.

While it is usually considered Ragnar had two or three wives, there is one other woman that needs to be mentioned in this section.

SWANLOGA

While many people have heard of Lagertha, Thora, and Aslaug as wives of Ragnar, another wife is mentioned in Saxo Grammaticus' *Gesta Danorum*. This wife's name is Swanloga and is mentioned only twice in the ninth book of the *Gesta Danorum*.

The first time this wife is disclosed is not long after Thora dies. Ragnar, having been overcome by grief, takes to warfare. Thanks to this sorrow spurring him on, Ragnar enacts a new law in his land that sees every father across the land sending their "most contemptible"[20] son or any lazy slave into service for Ragnar. This army is devised to prove that even the "feeblest of the Danish Race were better than the strongest men of other nations."[21]

This army then goes on to kill King Hame, and many of the earls of Scotland and Pictland. This causes conflict and many rally to the side of a Viking man named Harald. This dispute plays out like the previous one that involved Ragnar and Lagertha, leading the reader to wonder if Saxo is repeating the same story just from a differing viewpoint or region of the time.

---

[20] Grammaticus, S. (2016). *The Danish History Books I-X*. [e-book]. Perennial Press. Available through: <https://www.amazon.com/Danish-History-Books-I-IX-ebook/dp/B01BRM2VFQ/> [Accessed: 2017].
[21] Grammaticus, S. (2016). *The Danish History Books I-X*. [e-book]. Perennial Press. Available through: <https://www.amazon.com/Danish-History-Books-I-IX-ebook/dp/B01BRM2VFQ/> [Accessed: 2017].

After this conflict, Ragnar hears that the father of his wife, Thora, has been killed and his sons robbed of their inheritance rights. As a result of this, Ragnar seeks the aid of some of his sons.

> "He besought the aid of the brothers Biorn, Fridleif, and Ragbard (for Ragnald, Hwitserk, and Erik, his sons by Swanloga, had not yet reached the age of bearing arms), and went to Sweden."[22]

This is the first time his wife, Swanloga, is mentioned. So, who is this woman and where did she suddenly appear from? Perhaps by unravelling the heritage of Ragnar's children, her identity will be revealed.

Previously, Saxo had listed Fridleif as the son of Lagertha, and Biorn (Bjorn) as the son of Aslaug. Ragbard has not been mentioned, although it is very possible a misspelling of Thora's son, Radbard. The *Gesta Danorum* lists Thora's sons as Radbard and Dunwat, however, in the saga's her sons are listed as Agnar and Eirik (or Eirek). Consequently, it is possible that Erik could be a misspelling of Eirik, indicating that perhaps Saxo has mixed up some of Ragnar's children with their mothers.

This is not the first time this happens in the ninth book of the *Gesta Danorum* either. Thora is listed as having two sons to Ragnar, but those children also having other brothers: Siward, Biorn, Agnar, and Iwar. Those names seem familiar for a reason. After all, some of them are usually credited with being the children of Aslaug. So, could Hwitserk be a misspelling of Hvitserk, and, place this child as one of Aslaug's?

---

[22] Grammaticus, S. (2016). *The Danish History Books I-X*. [e-book]. Perennial Press. Available through: <https://www.amazon.com/Danish-History-Books-I-IX-ebook/dp/B01BRM2VFQ/> [Accessed: 2017].

If this is the case, then two of Swanloga's children can be accredited to two of Ragnar's other wives. Potentially, Ragnald could also be a different spelling for one of Aslaug's sons, Rognvald, who is mentioned in the *Tale of Ragnar's Sons.*

So, could Swanloga be another name for Aslaug then? After all, in the *Saga of Ragnar Lodbrok and his Sons*, Aslaug also goes by the names of Kraka and Randalin, indicating she may also have another moniker in Swanloga. If so, this would mean Ragnald and Hwitserk were her sons in the *Gesta Danorum.* Some people suspect this is the case, meaning the above passage is referencing Aslaug and not another wife.

Further on in the *Gesta Danorum*, there is another reference to Swanloga. This time, it talks about her death. This event occurs after the death of Thora's sons and as a result of a battle between Ragnar and King Murial from the Orkneys.

> "[Ragnar] returned to Denmark, and found that his wife Swanloga had in the meantime died of disease."[23]

After hearing this news, Ragnar goes into a deep despair and seeks medicine for his grief and loneliness. Already, this woman's story is starting to parallel another of Ragnar's wives: Thora. So, could Saxo be referring to Thora here and has attributed her with a different name? Unfortunately, it is not clear and readers of the *Gesta Danorum* can only make their own assumptions from the passages provided.

While this concludes the section on Ragnar's wives, there are still other women in his life that need mentioning.

---

[23] Grammaticus, S. (2016). *The Danish History Books I-X.* [e-book]. Perennial Press. Available through: <https://www.amazon.com/Danish-History-Books-I-IX-ebook/dp/B01BRM2VFQ/> [Accessed: 2017].

THE OTHER WOMEN

ɪNGIBJORG

Ingibjorg is the daughter of Eystein, from Sweden. Some texts place Eystein as simply an earl placed in charge of Sweden by Ragnar to act as his regent for the area. Others place Eystein (also known as Eystein Beli) as the outright king of Sweden.

There are also two versions of events in regard to Ragnar and Eystein. One is that Ragnar placed Eystein as the regent of Sweden because he was jealous of his own sons and wanted Eystein to protect the country from them. Even with this tactic, Eystein still ends up in a battle with Ragnar's sons. The other version involves Eystein's daughter, Ingibjorg.

In the *Saga of Ragnar Lodbrok and his Sons*, Eystein battles Ragnar's sons as a result of a betrothal made between Ragnar and Eystein's daughter, Ingibjorg. The reason for this betrothal is because Aslaug had not been revealed as Sigurd and Brynhildr's daughter yet and many thought Ragnar had married well below his standing with the peasant known as Kraka.

When Kraka found out about this betrothal, she revealed her identity. Ragnar immediately broke off his betrothal to Ingibjorg and this created conflict between Ragnar and Eystein. As a result of this, Ragnar's sons, Eirik and Agnar, went to Sweden to defend their father and Aslaug. Thora's sons were killed in the process before Ivar led an army to Sweden and defeated Eystein.

Prior to all this, Ingibjorg is considered to be the most beautiful of all women. It is unclear from the text if this applies just to Sweden, or if it covers all of Scandinavia at the time.

During the early years and leading up to his daughter's betrothal, Eystein and Ragnar were considered great friends. They would take turns to visit each other every year, so it can be assumed that Ragnar and Ingibjorg could have known each other reasonably well.

Once again, it is unclear what Ingibjorg thought about Ragnar as the texts don't mention anything from her perspective. All that is known is that she served his drinks during the feast in which he became betrothed to Ragnar, so it could be said she knew about the impending betrothal or may have had a part to play in ensnaring him in this manner.

While Ragnar and Ingibjorg were betrothed to each other, they were not actually married. It is suggested the betrothal would last for a considerable length of time, so it could be assumed from this that perhaps Ingibjorg was still too young to wed.

After this event, Ragnar travelled home and is confronted by Aslaug about his betrothal. While the events unfold as listed above, Ingibjorg is not mentioned after this point and it is unclear what becomes of her after her father is killed by Ivar's army.

And so her involvement with Ragnar concludes here. However, there is one more woman who needs to be mentioned in regard to Ragnar's story. This woman, unfortunately, no longer has a recorded name and so must be referenced by the son she and Ragnar produced.

UBBE'S MOTHER

In the *Gesta Danorum*, after Ragnar attacked and killed Sorle, who took Sweden from his sons after Herodd died, he decided to rest a while from wars. During this time, he managed to "fall deeply in love with a certain woman."[24] While this woman seems to have captivated Ragnar, Saxo has decided not to include her name. However, we do know that her father was called Esbern.

Ragnar goes out of his way to impress this woman's father in an effort to approach and win the woman's affections. This could indicate that this woman was not as interested in Ragnar as he was in her.

This time around, in order to win this woman over, Ragnar invites Esbern to many banquets and treats him lavishly. It could be suggested, through the passage involving the persuasion of Esbern that perhaps he and his daughter were not of a high enough standing as Ragnar is since Ragnar often "paid him the respect of rising."[25] He also "comforted"[26] him with gifts, perhaps an indication this family was not very

---

[24] Grammaticus, S. (2016). *The Danish History Books I-X*. [e-book]. Perennial Press. Available through: <https://www.amazon.com/Danish-History-Books-I-IX-ebook/dp/B01BRM2VFQ/> [Accessed: 2017].

[25] Grammaticus, S. (2016). *The Danish History Books I-X*. [e-book]. Perennial Press. Available through: <https://www.amazon.com/Danish-History-Books-I-IX-ebook/dp/B01BRM2VFQ/> [Accessed: 2017].

[26] Grammaticus, S. (2016). *The Danish History Books I-X*. [e-book]. Perennial Press. Available through: <https://www.amazon.com/Danish-History-Books-I-IX-ebook/dp/B01BRM2VFQ/> [Accessed: 2017].

wealthy. Later in the *Gesta Danorum*, it is mentioned that they live in a farmhouse and the daughter is seen doing manual work, so this assumption could be correct.

In fact, after a while, Esbern starts to realise that perhaps Ragnar is only being nice to him to win the affection of his daughter. After this point, Esbern has his daughter watched more closely in an indication and Ragnar has to be cleverer in his attempts to woo her.

So, what does Ragnar do at this point? He dresses himself in women's clothing because he is convinced by the consent of Esbern's daughter of him. He then pretended to be a woman at her side, even taking on menial tasks to complete the picture he was a maiden and not a king.

That night Ragnar makes advances on this woman and she ultimately complies with his wishes.

It is not long after this that it is noticed this woman is now pregnant. Esbern is suitably outraged at the fact his daughter has been defiled and asks her who the man was. She insists that she had "no one to share her bed except her handmaiden."[27] Not knowing what to do, Esbern turns "the affair over to the king to search into."[28]

It is at this point in the tale that Ragnar reveals himself as being the father of the unborn child in order to save the servant of Ubbe's mother who is being "branded with an extraordinary charge." Presumably, this means the servant did not prevent an act that resulted in pregnancy. Ragnar then announces the child will be born to his line and requests the child be named Ubbe.

[27] Grammaticus, S. (2016). *The Danish History Books I-X*. [e-book]. Perennial Press. Available through: <https://www.amazon.com/Danish-History-Books-I-IX-ebook/dp/B01BRM2VFQ/> [Accessed: 2017].
[28] Grammaticus, S. (2016). *The Danish History Books I-X*. [e-book]. Perennial Press. Available through: <https://www.amazon.com/Danish-History-Books-I-IX-ebook/dp/B01BRM2VFQ/> [Accessed: 2017].

Later, when Ubbe has grown somewhat, it is noted that he loves his mother dearly, especially considering she managed to woo someone of higher standing than her. However, he refuses to show any respect for his father who had "stooped to a union too lowly."[29]

While Ubbe may not respect his father for his actions with his mother, he does later on go an expedition with Ragnar to help defeat the Hellespont king, Dia. Then follows a somewhat turbulent relationship between Ubbe and his father. There are several power plays and Ragnar ends up killing Ubbe's grandfather, Esbern.

After this point in the *Gesta Danorum*, Ubbe's mother is never mentioned again.

This also concludes the list of women in which Ragnar was involved. If you would like to find out more about Ragnar and the women who loved him, please consider the following list of historical sources for their stories.

[29] Grammaticus, S. (2016). *The Danish History Books I-X*. [e-book]. Perennial Press. Available through: <https://www.amazon.com/Danish-History-Books-I-IX-ebook/dp/B01BRM2VFQ/> [Accessed: 2017].

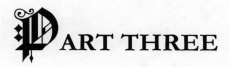

PART THREE

LOOKING FURTHER INTO THE WORLD OF THE VIKINGS

HISTORICAL SOURCES

When approaching the historical sources in regard to Viking history, historians have to battle many obstacles.

There are various sources of information from many different places. Some are English sources, others from the areas the Vikings originated from. Each of these sources were written hundreds of years ago, and, therefore, have to be translated and interpreted not only because of the language, but because of the cultural differences at the time.

Besides the obvious complications that arise form translating older versions of languages, there can be many varied interpretation errors. Of course, another complication with translating from old sources, is matching up various names.

Then, to add even more dimension, one needs to be aware that several characters within the Vikings history have the same name. Siward is an excellent example of this. Siward was Ragnar's grandfather, but Ragnar's father was also Siward. In addition, traditionally, Ragnar is known to have a son, Sigurd, which is a variant of the spelling of Siward. So, depending on which translation you might be reading, you could encounter three characters all with the same name. In addition, sometimes, it is very hard to interpret from the original source just who the author might be talking about. A prime example of this is the very start of the ninth book of the *Gesta Danorum* when it appears Saxo is talking about three different Siwards, but might only be talking about two. Herald is another example of a common Viking name that could be attributed to several different people.

Another factor to consider is, in regard to the written word, the Vikings did not record their history and lore like the Christians did. Consequently, it is difficult to find many sources from the Viking era that are written down. The Viking culture was handed down orally and, besides the runes, there was no written language. Most of the Viking sagas have originated from poems and oral retellings, meaning it is unclear how the stories originally began and how much has changed over time with each generation of retellings. However, there are a few sources from territories associated with the Vikings, for example, the Icelandic sagas.

Another obstacle involved with the written lore of the Vikings as recorded by Viking and non-Viking sources alike is the fact these tales were not written down until after the events occurred. In some cases, the tales of the Vikings were written down two hundred years, or more, after the events took place.

While it is fantastic someone took the time to record the feats of the Vikings, once again, it is impossible to gauge how much these stories may have changed and evolved over the course of time.

Regardless of when these stories were written down, they are now the only historical sources available for the Viking Era. While historians use them to unravel the past, they are also cautious in the knowledge that many of these stories are steeped in hearsay. In addition, they have evolved over time to become the stories we now know. In some cases, over various sources, there appears to be an overlapping of events and different versions of stories. This could indicate that the event did occur, but was written down by different sources according to the local knowledge of the event or the writer's interpretation of the event. While this can be confusing to those trying to discover the truth, it does also add a certain level of authenticity to a tale if it is recorded in different sources, despite the differences. The authenticity then comes from the shared parts of the different versions.

So, what are these historical sources?

The following is a list of some of the historical manuscripts used in relation to deciphering the history of Ragnar and the women he was involved with that you might want to peruse. This is by no means a concise or complete reading list on the Vikings, merely a starting point based on the stories involving Ragnar Lodbrok.

Gesta Danorum by Saxo Grammaticus

Historically, this set of sixteen books, also known as the *History of the Danes*, were written some time before 1208. It is unclear when the completion date was. The first nine books in this series consist of Old Norse mythology. The remainder deal with medieval history. Only four fragments still exist of the original manuscripts: the Angers Fragment, Lassen Fragment, Kall-Rasmussen Fragment and Plesner Fragment. However, it is only the Angers Fragment that can be attributed to having Saxo's handwriting. Complete later editions of these works date from 1275. Interesting to note is the fact William Shakespeare based his play, *Hamlet*, on a story from the *Gesta Danorum* about Amleth, the Prince of Denmark.

Saxo Grammaticus was a Danish scholar who was encouraged to write the history of the Danes by Absalon, Archbishop of Lund. Some of the *Gesta Danorum* was written in accordance with old Icelandic sagas as well as the parts of history the Archbishop was directly involved with. At times, his religious bias is found within the *Gesta Danorum*, adding further weight to the fact it might not be truly representative of the original sagas.

The Prose Edda by Snorri Sturluson

Also called *Snorri's Edda*, *Younger Edda*, or, simply, *Edda*, is a collection of works written by Snorri in Iceland in the early 13th century (estimated sometime around 1220). This means this source is likely more biased toward Viking events, than English or Christian sources. While not necessarily more accurate, it is certainly more sympathetic to the Vikings, their culture and beliefs.

Codex Regius

The *Codex Regius* is thought to have been written sometime in the 1270s, but it is not until 1643 when the book became more commonly known. Originally, when *The Prose Edda* was the only Edda available, some scholars suggested there was an older body of works containing the full versions of the pagan poems Snorri quoted. When the *Codex Regius* was discovered, many scholars saw this as proof of this original speculation.

The *Codex Regius* and the *Poetic Edda* has been used interchangeably at times, leading to some confusion to those who are starting out in their endeavour to learn about the history of the Vikings. Others prefer to cite the *Codex Regius* as the original source of the *Poetic Edda*. The two have been included separately in this instance to let the reader know when they come across mentions of these tomes they are often in reference to the same, or similar, manuscript.

The Poetic Edda

This body of work is likely based on the *Codex Regius* and there is some evidence to suggest this work could also be called the *Elder Edda* in placement of the *Codex Regius*. As stated above, *The Poetic Edda* and the *Codex Regius* are considered interchangeable, so, if you come across people talking about either sources and they sound surprisingly similar, this is the reason for it.

The Sagas

The sagas usually refer to a collection of Icelandic works that were written down largely in the 12th through to the 14th centuries, although, sometimes people will describe all sources about the Viking tales as "the sagas." Once again, the Icelandic sagas are stories based on much older tales regarding the migration period during the 5th and 6th centuries and could be considered romanticised versions of the original tales. According to the website, AllScandinavia.com, there are about forty sagas in total, ranging in length from a few pages up to 400 pages.

Some of these sagas have been broken up and published under various sources. *The Saga of the Volsungs*, also known as the *Völsunga saga*, is a selection based directly on the Völsung clan that included such characters as Sigurd and Brynhild, the parents of Ragnar's wife, Aslaug.

The *Tale of Ragnar Lodbrok* is considered a sequel to the *Saga of the Volsungs*. It tells of Ragnar's marriages to Thora and Aslaug as well as the feats of his sons. The *Tale of Ragnar Lodbrok* also deals with his death at the hands of King Ælla.

Nowell Codex

The *Nowell Codex* contains the famous poem, *Beowulf*. This poem is set in Scandinavia and was written sometime between the 8th and the early 11th century.

Heimskringla

Also known as *The Lives of the Norse Kings*, this book was written by Snorri Sturluson in Iceland in the early 13th century (estimated sometime around 1230). This book is a collection of sagas about the Norwegian kings dating from the early Swedish Yngling dynasty through to Harald Fairhair's rule in the 9th century and ending with the death of Eystein Meyla in 1177. It is unclear exactly which sources Snorri used to write this book, but the suggestion is that many stories came from older Scandinavian poems and earlier kings' sagas. Snorri also lists the now lost work of *Hryggjarstkki* as one of his sources.

Anglo Saxon Chronicle

This chronicle was written sometime late in the 9th century and was being actively updated as late as 1154. This makes it, surprisingly, a fairly accurate source for some events involving the Vikings due to the fact it is, at times, written quite close to actual events as they occur. It is likely this document was originally written in Wessex, England during the reign of Alfred the Great, a man who was directly involved with the Vikings and their conquests. Alfred is usually credited as one of the authors of this document.

While this is an English source, several events it contains involves the Vikings and their interactions with the English.

ᚠ

As you can see, these sources occur around the time of the Viking era, however, are not usually sources from the early stages of it. While they are some of the only sources known on the Viking era, it must be noted that there may be a level of both bias and error in these sources along with the truth. Nevertheless, without these sources, there would be none of the myths and legends about the Vikings we know of today. Therefore, it is these sources that will be used to delve into the truth behind the Viking characters and the people around them.

REFERENCES

When one starts to delve into the history of the Vikings, it seems there are only a few major sources. However, myriad resources as well as various translations and scholarly tomes and articles delve into various stories involving the Vikings.

Therefore, this account of Ragnar's romances has not been a simple one. Below is the list of resources I have used in preparation of *Ragnar and the Women Who Loved Him*.

Some of these texts, being so old, fall outside of copyright, so are freely accessible online. Many of these texts can also be found as scanned documents on archive.org or as reproduced documents on Project Gutenberg. Both sites offer various formats to either view or download each item.

Archive.org is an online resource where out of copyright books, documents, letters, video, etc. have been scanned, uploaded and, where required, digitalised, by Google so that people can access these resources easily.

Project Gutenberg is another online resource aiming to bring out of copyright tomes within the reach of everyone. If you prefer to use this resource, you can simply visit gutenberg.org and start searching.

Anglo Saxon Chronicle. Edited from the translation in *Monumenta Historica Britanica and Other Versions* by the Late J. A. Giles D C.L. New Edition, (1914). London G. Bell and Sons, Ltd.

Danish History Books I-X, The. Grammaticus, S. (2016). Perennial Press This edition includes the original copy of the *Gesta Danorum* from the version available free online at the Gutenberg Project that has been translated by Oliver Elton (Norroena Society, New York, 1905) and edited, proofed, and prepared by Douglas B. Killings.

Heimskringla: A History of the Norse Kings. Sturluson, S., Monsen, E. (translated), and Smith, A. (New York, 1932). Dover Publications, Inc.

Icelandic Sagas. These sources are many and varied. The best place to start researching this source is probably the website, Icelandic Saga Database (http://www.sagadb.org/). It must be noted however, that not all of the sagas listed on this website are available in English.

Nowell Codex. Cotton MS Vitellius A XV. Each component of the volume contained within the Nowell Codex was acquired by Sir Robert Bruce Cotton (b. 1571, d. 1631). This collection was expanded on by his son, Sir Thomas Cotton (b. 1594, d. 1662), and grandson, Sir John Cotton (b. 1621, d. 1702). The entire collection was then bequeathed to trustees "for Publick Use and Advantage." According to the British Library, who hold the original documents, the previous ownership of the respective parts is as follows:(i) [f 1]: made in England (ii) f 3: made in England (iii) ff 4–93: made in England; owned by Southwick Priory (Hampshire) (iv) ff 94–209: made in England; owned by Laurence Nowell (d. c. 1570).

Poetic Edda, The. Bellows, H. (translated) (New York, 1923) The American-Scandinavian Foundation. As discussed earlier in the section on sources used, *The Poetic Edda* can be considered interchangeable with another source called the *Codex Regius.*

Prose Edda, The. Sturluson, S., Gilchrist, A. (1916). Brodeur.

Saga of the Volsungs, The. Bylock, J. (translated). (United States, 1990). Penguin Classics.

Sagas of Ragnar Lodbrok, The, Waggoner, B. (Connecticut, 2009). The Troth.

Viking Poetry of Love and War. Jesch, J. (2013). The British Museum Press.

SNEAK PEEK AT BOOK #2

VIKINGS: THE TRUTH ABOUT LAGERTHA AND RAGNAR

PROLOGUE

The slope was slippery as Lagertha fought her way up the steep incline to the wise woman's hut. Wind sliced through her with a sharpness that felt like flint first thing in the morning. Glancing skyward, she watched the dark clouds roil and seethe. The drops hit her a moment later. She grunted, knowing her treacherous journey was about to get even more difficult.

The seidhr's cabin was just ahead. She knew this, but still carefully picked her way along the narrow path. Last winter, her uncle had slipped and broken his ankle here, so haste was not an option.

The hut was old, older than time the seidhr had told her when she was a child and wavering over the sagas she heard told and retold over the long winter months. Sensing her distraction, their seidhr told the children gathered around the large fire in the centre of her parent's longhouse the story of how she had become the wise woman for their village.

But now it was time to watch her footing and not be lost in her childhood memories. There was a question to ask and she would not sleep well until it had been answered. Or, perhaps she would sleep worse. Shaking her head to clear that last thought, she dug her nails into the branch at her side. Once a sapling, as people climbed, the tree had died and was now smooth and well weathered from those that had travelled before her and clasped onto it for support.

Each step she took was one her ancestors had already taken before her. It was a comfort. She looked skyward as the thunder cracked overhead and brightened her way for a moment. A thank you was mumbled under her breath to the mighty Thor. A second of bright light was a good sign, she decided.

Her feet slipped as the rain steadily increased until she could not tell where each drop landed. Still she fought her way forward. The journey was hard, but there was a reason for that. A question asked of the wise woman was always a weighty decision. The seidhr had no time for stupid questions asked randomly. Instead, the long, difficult trek was supposed to clear the mind and help a person decide if their query was important enough to warrant the journey.

"Sweet Lagertha," the old woman said as she scratched on the door. "Why are you here?"

"I have a question for you." Lagertha sat at the wise woman's feet, laying out a selection of goods for an offering. The gods would not speak through the woman if she didn't have an equal valued gift for them.

Bony fingers reached out, touching the cloth, the white round stone that reminded Lagertha of the moon, the salted fish, and the withered roots that were the best of what she still had stored. It had been a long winter after all. The seidhr wouldn't take these blessings on Lagertha's behalf to present to the gods. Instead, she would use them to help guide her as she sought an answer from them. It acted as a blessing, of sorts. Lagertha would then take the items to another place, to make her own personal offering to the gods.

"Everyone is always asking questions." The seidhr ran the dried herbs under her nose, the movement releasing the dusty scent of sage that hung in the air briefly, before it tangled with the wood smoke and dissipated.

"I need to know who I will marry," Lagertha asked, always direct. It was in her nature. She couldn't see the point of wasting hers or the seidhr's time with small talk.

"Ah, you ask of marriage." The seidhr rocked back slowly onto her feet before returning the sage to the other offerings. Her knotted joints stiff with age, made the task an effort. "All women seem to want to know of their future husbands."

Lagertha waited. The woman would answer her question, or not. If she seemed impatient, the answer would only be delayed. Patience was something she always struggled with and their village seidhr knew this. Any chance she could help teach her a lesson, she would. Lagertha bit at the inside of her cheek and tucked her hands underneath her robe to hide how clenched they were. It wasn't that she feared getting married, it was just that she hated not having much of a choice in it. She curbed her patience further still by concentrating on the seidhr's features, her weathered face, and the jumble of grey hair barely contained within their braids. The woman was beautiful, even now, but her beauty was like old leather, refined, functional, yet cracked with age.

"Of all the questions I get asked, Lagertha, I think the most common is from young women such as yourself asking about who they will wed." The seidhr poked a gnarled stick at the fire, helping the flames dance higher in the dim room. "I see their fear, their hope, and their excitement. However, I do not see that on your face, Lagertha. Why is that so?"

Lagertha lowered her gaze. What was it she felt, she wondered? It was a question she had to ask. But it wasn't because she wanted a husband, or for her adult life to begin. Instead, she was hoping the seidhr would say there would be no one. That her life would be her own and not belong to someone else.

"I don't need a husband." Lagertha set her jaw and raised her steely gaze to meet firmly with the woman across from her.

"You may not, my dear. However, your family does."

"I know." Neither of them blinked as the silence lengthened between them. Lagertha finally sighed. "Can you tell me if I will marry then?"

More silence. Finally, she lowered her eyes rather than have the wise woman bear down into her mind any longer.

"Let me have a look for you."

Lagertha expelled a long steady breath, trying to silence it rather than alert the seidhr to her relief.

As she left, Lagertha held her sacred offerings close to her chest. She was relieved to know she would eventually rule on her own, having no man preside over her. However, knowing she would be married thrice indicated she would have a very long wait to endure before she could step out from the weight of responsibility, perhaps nearly a whole lifetime.

She could hear the water before she saw the waterfall. A thin sliver cascaded from high above and splattered down over the rocks, landing, finally, in a small pool that quickly disappeared into jagged rocks. It was not the prettiest place to worship, here in the land known for its waterfalls, but it was her favourite.

Placing the items down on the flat rock that had seen generations of offerings and sacrifices, she arranged each item carefully. She gave her blessing to the wight that resided there, in the air, and the water and the ground that she walked upon.

Her destiny reached out with long slender fingers, eager to clasp her and pull her forward into her predestined future.

Chapter 1: IN THE BEGINNING

Lagertha's tale truly begins with one king overthrowing another. As with all great tales, it starts with a fierce battle. Siward the rightful ruler of Norway was attacked and brutally slain by Fro, the king of Sweden.

With this event came great calamity. In the midst of the upheaval, as was the way of cruel leaders wishing to set an example, or to display their dominance, the female kinfolk and the wives of his male kinfolk were sent into servitude. This was a more terrifying fate than death for some. For others, a new hell in which they must endure merely because they were women and had little say in their lives other than with a knife to end it all.

The servitude they had to endure was that of prostitution.

Lagertha took her fall from standing as well as she could. She fought valiantly when their longhouse was surrounded, but it was hard to retaliate against a surprise attack, and Lagertha had let her training slip. Being a noble woman and having idle time on her hands had softened her. When Fro's men attacked, Lagertha had grabbed for a sword. It was an old reflex, she discovered, but a sword was no longer by her side. In fact, she couldn't remember where her last sword was. Probably, it was still back at her mother's house, left behind after she married; a forgotten relic from her youth. It was a mistake she would never make again she vowed every night as men pounded into her flesh.

As a result, Lagertha closed her eyes when she needed to and bore the brunt of aggression when it came. Some men were worse than others, a quick cuff here, as opposed to a bloodied nose there. Either way, Fro didn't care, except for when the abuse was so bad a woman was temporarily unproductive.

She knew she could fight her way out of the situation, but didn't for fear of even worse living conditions than those she was already in. There was also the constant threat that her wrongdoings would impact on the other women around her. It was this alone that kept her in line and obedient. Instead, she bade her time.

Geir, her husband, was dead. Yet she clung to the seidhr's prophecy that there would be another husband on the horizon for her. Not that she looked forward to yet another man to stand over her, but it surely meant that this current level of suffering would end.

Those around her didn't have that luxury. Some killed themselves rather than endure their fate. Others had run, fleeing for their lives. It was when these women were captured and returned that Lagertha truly understood suffering. Not only were the escapees punished, the other women were as well. Some of those escapees were never found again, though. Where they went Lagertha didn't know. Who would even take them in now Siward was dead and Fro was in charge? They were shamed women, leftovers from a past ruler. Unless someone usurped Fro and set them free, they all had little choice. It was the brothel or it was death.

Lagertha's only hope was that her next husband wasn't one of the men who frequented her or, worse still, a regular to one of the women she worked beside.

Every night as the moon rose, Lagertha begged its personification, Mani, for a change in her circumstance. While she knew her fate was predestined, she still offered what she could by way of sacrifice in the hope that the existence she now lived was only temporary, or that Mani would take pity on her and somehow alter it.

Considering what the seidhr had told her though, she was confident her lot would change at some point in time. Perhaps, with a new husband, and a change of circumstance, she would have the opportunity to break free of him, to be liberated from constraint. In addition, her second husband would place her that much closer to her third. And, with him, eventually, freedom would come.

As she gazed up at the moon, she dreamed and planned her life ahead of her. The moon would always shine bright, even when the inevitable knock at the door heralded Lagertha's first customer each night, disappearing as it was replaced with the brutish lust of the man on top of her.

Chapter 2: LAGERTHA

"Lagertha, your customer is here." Gunnvor nodded her head and averted her eyes. Their life was a special kind of torture now, and eye contact only made it worse.

Lagertha sighed as she raised herself from her sleeping place. She left the room shared with five other women and entered the hut where she worked. Pushing aside the leather hide door, she was surprised to see a familiar face.

"What are you doing here, Herodd?" She paused at the doorway, letting the hide fall behind her. The room was dim even with the small fire burning. Still, she knew that face. She had spoken to him, even if it had only been a few times and over innocuous things at a gathering of family members. He was a relative of Geir, who had travelled far from home to explore new lands when Fro took over. Lagertha knew this because they had discussed his upcoming travel the last time they met. Lagertha had also commented on his new shield, with its elaborate design. Herodd had seemed surprised when she knew of such things.

Lagertha's voice was low, wavering a little, not sure she wanted to be doing this with one of her husband's relatives. Every day, it seemed, she found herself thinking she had finally reached the absolute worst of the situation. However, having a man standing in front of her now, a man whom she actually knew before Siward was killed, well, that really might be the worst thing ever, she decided.

The last time they met, Lagertha also discussed crops with him. She had been curious and asked him to keep an eye out for strange and exotic foods during his travels, things that might be suited to grow in their climate. For a moment, she wanted to ask if he'd bought any seeds back with him, forgetting, entirely, the situation she was currently in.

"Shh, they can't realise we know of each other. For both our sakes."

Lagertha ducked her head. Kneeling down, she warmed her frigid hands over the fire as she tried to work out how to approach this man she knew, yet found she didn't know considering where he was and what she was now used for.

"What would you like?" she asked, louder this time so the men outside could hear her.

Herodd approached. Lagertha automatically leaned back on her heels, pulling herself away from him. After all this time, her new life didn't sit comfortably with her upbringing or standing. Sometimes men hit her for this small infraction. Other times they were rough with her to compensate for her obvious aversion to them. Only a few were kind or backed off and allowed her to approach at her own pace. None had ever been kind enough to leave her entirely alone though.

This man, however, stared across the fire at her for the longest time.

"Drop your gown." He spoke roughly as if he didn't have time to be coy. Lagertha's blooming hope he might not be there for the usual reason withered. She stood, raising her eyes and stared at him as she reached for the drawstring to her robe. A quick shake of his head made her pause.

"Come here."

Lagertha moved around the fire, her hands still clutching at her neckline. She sat down on the sleeping ledge. The rough furs rumpled between them smelled of sex, sweat, and the tang of coarse wine. To her this was what regret and despair smelled like.

The man leaned in as if to kiss the crook of her neck. Instead, he whispered, his breath tickling her ear.

"Ragnar knows of your plight. He is coming. There is a plan."

Lagertha yelped and clapped one hand over her mouth as she tried to swallow the sound back down. Had she heard him right? There was a plan? She almost cried with relief.

"But, why did you come to me? I do not know Ragnar." Lagertha was surprised the king even knew of her existence.

"He doesn't, but I do. I still remember that conversation we had about shields and swordplay. When he wanted to know if there were any warriors among the ranks, I immediately thought of you."

She had heard of Ragnar, an arrogant young king who was the grandson of Siward. He was known for his progressive ways and womanising. The last time she paid any attention to gossip, Ragnar had been involved with a woman who came from nothing, but was supposed to be of high-standing.

Regardless of whether he was involved with this woman now, Lagertha still anticipated he would be after payment of the flesh for their safety. She didn't care. It would be worth it for her freedom from this wretched place. What was one last usage of her body if it meant she was finally free?

"What do we need to do?"

"When the time comes, you must be ready." He whispered it into her ear so close she could feel the dampness of his hissing breath. "I will return when Ragnar is near."

She shivered. It would be a long wait, but her freedom was coming. Lagertha swallowed hard and held back her emotion. Now was not the time to seem weak.

"Can any of you defend yourselves?" he asked.

"I can, others will try. We are all eager to be free of this wretched place."

"Good. I will leave you now. Speak only to those who you trust, Fro doesn't need to be alerted that Ragnar is on his way."

Chapter 3: LAGERTHA

"He's really coming?" Astrid asked.

It had been a regular refrain for the past month. Lagertha tried hard not to roll her eyes at the stupid girl. To be honest, Astrid was probably best suited to the role of whore or concubine rather than warrior, but Lagertha didn't have much choice in her army.

Of course, if everything went according to plan she wouldn't need an army and these women would never have to be tested in blood.

"He's really coming, but we need to be smart about this. Already I am sure Fro suspects something. He knows we are not as despondent about being here. We need to play our part a bit better."

"When will he get here?" Another question she was sick of hearing.

"I don't know. As soon as I get word, I'll tell you, you know that. But we won't know until Ragnar is actually here and his army is in place. It's safest that way."

Lagertha thought about the man who was coming to rescue them: Ragnar. She knew he was young. He was older than she was, for sure, but still young enough for her to question his authority and whether he could lead an army.

She had heard of how he became a king from a very young age, probably too tender an age, she figured. Regardless, he had still rallied to get armies to follow him. Yet, she also knew of how tales grew over time. He could just as likely be a drunkard or a fool as the great leader everyone knew.

She had seen him once before, not long after she wed Geir. At the time, Ragnar had toyed with every woman present. Lagertha was unsure she wanted to meet with the man again. He was fine to look upon, in fact, she had gazed at him long enough her husband noticed and pointed it out. It was the first time he cuffed her. It certainly wasn't the stupidest reason he had to hit her either. As a result, she didn't cry so much when Fro lopped her husband down.

"Has everyone got enough clothes?" Lagertha asked.

They were all nervous; their very lives depended on this rescue.

It had been hard to steal men's clothing without alerting anyone. The small items were easier. But even they were sometimes noted as missing. The poor woman in charge of washing Fro and his army's clothes was punished more than once for "ruining" men's shirts. She took the beatings in her stride, knowing she would have her chance for revenge if all went according to plan and Ragnar really did show up.

"We have enough, Lagertha, you know that. It's the waiting that's the worst."

"No, Fro's uncle is the worst."

The women laughed. Fro's uncle was old and smelled like turnips and soured sweat. He really was the worst because he also liked his whores to go down on him for the longest time. And his balls smelled even worse than the rest of him.

You can purchase *Vikings: The Truth about Lagertha and Ragnar* via Amazon.

If you enjoyed this book, please make sure to leave a review on Amazon and Goodreads. A long review is not needed, just adding a short sentence or two helps other potential readers find this book.

BOOKS BY RACHEL TSOUMBAKOS

Historical Fiction/Fantasy
Ragnar and the Women Who Loved Him (Viking Secrets #0)
Vikings: The Truth about Lagertha and Ragnar (Viking Secrets #1)
Vikings: The Truth about Thora and Ragnar (Viking Secrets #2)
Vikings: The Trouble with Ubbe's Mother (Viking Secrets #3)
Vikings: The Truth about Aslaug and Ragnar (Viking Secrets #4)
The Unnamed Warrior (Valkyrie Secrets #1)
Curse of the Valkyries (Valkyrie Secrets #2)
The Breaker of Curses (Valkyrie Secrets #3)
The Lost Viking (short story set in the same universe of Viking Secrets and Valkyrie Secrets)

Paranormal
Emeline and the Mutants
The Ring of Lost Souls
Metanoia
Unremembered Things

Horror
Zombie Apocalypse Now!

Make sure you sign up for my newsletter to find out when the next book in this series is due for release. You can do so here:
bit.ly/RachelNL

INDEX

A

Agnar, 33-4, 56, 58, 66, 67, 73
Aki, 59
Anglo Saxon Chronicle, 31-2, 87, 91
Aslaug, 34-8, 44-5, 53-63, 65-7, 72-3

B

Bjorn Ironside
    Biorn, 34, 66-7
Bjorn Ironside, 27, 35, 37, 58, 61, 66
Brynhildr, 59, 62, 72

C

Chronicle of Ireland, 27, 31
Codex Regius, 84-5, 92

D

Dunwat, 34, 56, 66

E

Eirik, 33, 56, 58, 66, 73
Esbern, 34, 75-7
Eystein, 61-2, 72-3

F

Frankish Annals, 27

G

Gesta Danorum, 26, 28, 30-6, 38, 44,
    46, 49-50, 52-8, 6-8, 75-7
Great Heathen Army, 31, 39

Grima, 59-60
Gyda, 27

H

Halfdan, 35
Harald, 31, 49, 65
Heimir, 59
Heimskringla, 32, 86
Hvitserk, 35, 37, 61, 67

I

Ingibjorg, 61-2, 72-3
Ivar the Boneless, 35, 37, 61
    Iwar, 34, 67

K

Kattegat, 27-8
King Aelle, 38-40, 63
King Fro, 46
King Hame, 65
King Herodd, 32-3, 49, 54-6, 75
Kraka (Aslaug), 37, 60-2, 67, 72

L

Lagertha, 27-28, 31-2, 34-6, 38, 44-5,
    58, 65-6

N

Nowell Codex, 86, 91

R

Radbard, 34, 56, 66
Ragnar, 26-50, 52-8, 60-3, 65-8, 72-7,
    81, 83, 86, 90, 92

Made in United States
Troutdale, OR
06/25/2024

20804608R00065